Ernesto Cira

Data Mining for Beginners: A Demystified Guide to Uncovering Hidden Insights in the Digital Age

Contents

1.

2.
    1.
    2.
    3.
    4.
    5.
3.
    1.
    2.
    3.
    4.
4.
    1.
    2.
    3.
    4.
5.
    1.
    2.
    3.
    4.
    5.
6.
    1.
    2.

Preface

In a world awash with data, hidden beneath the surface of countless spreadsheets, databases, and digital archives lies a treasure trove of insights waiting to be discovered. Welcome to the exhilarating journey of "Data Mining for Beginners." This book is your passport to the realm of data, where you will learn to wield powerful data mining tools to unveil hidden knowledge and turn information into action.

In an age where information is a currency of its own, the ability to extract meaningful patterns and make informed decisions is an invaluable skill. Whether you are a student taking your first steps into the world of data or a professional seeking to harness its transformative potential, this book is your trusted guide.

Chapter by chapter, we will venture into the heart of data mining, demystifying its principles and practices. We will delve into the intricacies of collecting, cleaning, and preparing data, transforming raw information into valuable insights. With the guidance of real-world case studies, you will witness the incredible impact data mining can have across diverse fields, from business and healthcare to science and beyond.

But data mining is not merely a technical pursuit but a journey that carries ethical responsibilities. Throughout this book, we will address the critical issues of privacy, bias, and transparency, ensuring that you emerge as a skilled data miner and an ethical practitioner.

As we journey through this text, we encourage you to engage actively with the material. Practice is the cornerstone of learning, and we have included practical exercises, examples, and challenges to sharpen your skills. Step by step, you will build the expertise needed to tackle real-world data mining projects with confidence.

This book is dedicated to all beginners embarking on this exciting voyage. Whether you are a student with boundless curiosity, a professional seeking to pivot your career, or anyone intrigued by the power of data, remember that every data mining journey begins with the first step. Embrace the challenges, savour the triumphs, and never cease to explore the limitless possibilities that data mining offers.

As you read the final words of this book, reflect on how far you've come. The knowledge you've gained will empower you to make a difference, uncover hidden truths, and contribute to a world where data is not just an asset but a force for good.

Thank you for choosing "Data Mining for Beginners." May your path in this fascinating field be illuminated with discovery, and may your passion for data mining continue to grow, enriching your life and the lives of those you touch.

With warm regards,

Ernesto   **Cira**

1

Chapter 1: Introduction to Data Mining

What is Data Mining?

An interdisciplinary branch of research called data mining, commonly referred to as knowledge discovery from data (KDD) focuses on extracting useful and previously unrecognized insights or patterns from huge databases. It entails sifting through enormous volumes of data using a variety of tools and algorithms to find hidden patterns, correlations, and trends before converting this raw data into informative and useful information.

Data mining involves:

1. **Pattern Discovery**: The fundamental goal of data mining is to find patterns in data. These patterns might appear as relationships, sequences, clusters, and prediction models, among others. For

instance, data mining in the retail industry may show that customers who buy product A are more likely to also buy product B.

2. **Data Types**: Both organized (such as databases and spreadsheets) and unstructured (such as text, photos, and videos) data may be mined. It is an effective tool for examining a variety of data sources because of its adaptability.

3. **Data Volume**: Data mining frequently works with substantial amounts of data, sometimes known as "big data." It is useful in the current era of data abundance because it can handle datasets that are too large for manual analysis.

4. **Data Preprocessing**: Data must be processed before data mining can take place. Cleaning up noisy data, dealing with missing values, and formatting data appropriately for analysis are just a few of the activities involved in this.

5. **Predictive Modeling**: Predictive modelling is one of the main goals of data mining. Building models that can categorize or make predictions based on previous data is required for this. For instance, determining if emails are spam or not, or forecasting client attrition in a telecom firm.

6. **Descriptive Modeling**: A component of data mining, descriptive modelling aims to summarize and characterize data trends. This can help you comprehend consumer behaviour, market trends, or any other domain-specific information better.

7. **Machine Learning Integration**: Data mining and machine learning frequently cross paths since many data mining approaches rely on machine learning algorithms for classification, regression, and pattern identification.

8. **Decision Support**: The data mining-derived information can be applied to a variety of decision-making processes. Data mining, for instance, may assist with illness prognosis and treatment planning in the healthcare industry.

Data mining: Why Is It Important?

Data mining is significant for many reasons, and as more and more massive volumes of data become accessible in the digital era, so has its importance.

Several factors make data mining crucial:

1. **Knowledge Discovery**: Using data mining, firms may glean important knowledge and insights from their data. Large datasets allow for the discovery of patterns, trends, and hidden linkages that may not be seen using more conventional approaches.

2. **Data-driven** decision-making is made possible through data mining. When making decisions in marketing, finance, operations, or strategic planning, businesses and organizations may leverage the insights gleaned via data mining. Decision-making processes become more effective and efficient as a result.

3. **Improved Predictive Analytics**: Predictive modelling may be done using data mining techniques like machine learning algorithms. This implies that businesses may predict present-day patterns and behaviour using data from the past. Businesses can foresee client preferences, equipment breakdowns, or stock market swings, for instance.

4. **Customer Insights**: Firms need to comprehend how customers behave. Data mining aids in the analysis of client data to pinpoint preferences, purchasing tendencies, and patterns. This data may be utilized to target marketing campaigns, raise consumer happiness, and keep devoted clients.

5. **Risk Management**: Data mining is crucial for risk assessment and management across a range of businesses, including banking and insurance. Examining trends in previous data, aids in identifying

possible hazards and fraudulent behaviours. This can prevent substantial financial losses for businesses.

6. **Healthcare and Medical Research**: In the healthcare industry, data mining is utilized to examine patient files and medical information to enhance patient care, spot illness trends, and create more potent medications. In addition, it can help with genome research and medication development.

7. **Scientific Research**: Across all fields, data mining is a critical component of scientific research. To gain new insights, confirm ideas, and enhance scientific knowledge, researchers might examine experimental data, simulations, and observational data.

8. **Industry analysis and competition intelligence**: Data mining enables companies to research industry trends, keep an eye on rivals, and spot untapped market niches. For creating powerful marketing strategies and establishing a competitive edge, this knowledge is priceless.

9. **Resource Allocation**: Data mining can optimize resource allocation, supply chain management, and production processes in sectors including logistics, transportation, and manufacturing. Costs are reduced as a result, and operational effectiveness is raised.

10. **Social and Behavioral Analysis**: In the social sciences, sentiment analysis, social networks, and human behaviour are all studied through data mining. For sociological and psychological

study, it can offer insights into how individuals interact, make decisions, and affect one another.

11. **Security and Fraud Detection**: Data mining plays a key role in identifying security risks and fraudulent activity across a range of industries, including cybersecurity, credit card fraud detection, and identity theft protection.

Applications of Data Mining:

Data mining is a potent method for sifting through enormous databases to find patterns, information, and insights that can be applied across a wide range of sectors and fields. Here are a few important uses for data mining:

1. **CRM (Customer Relationship Management) and marketing**

   - **client Segmentation**: Based on shared traits, data mining enables businesses to split their client base into various categories. This makes it possible for customized product suggestions and targeted marketing efforts.

   - **Churn Prediction**: By examining past data, data mining may pinpoint consumers who are most likely to churn (end doing business with a firm), enabling organizations to take preventative retention efforts.

2. Retail and E-commerce:

- **Market Basket Analysis:** Retailers employ data mining to identify relationships between items bought in combination. Cross-selling, marketing, and product placement all benefit from this knowledge.

- **Demand Forecasting**: Data mining can forecast future product demand, enabling merchants to manage their inventories and supply chains more effectively.

3. Healthcare:

- **illness Diagnosis and Prediction:** Patient records and medical data are analyzed using data mining to help with illness diagnosis, pinpoint populations at risk, and forecast disease outbreaks.

- **medication Discovery**: To find prospective medication candidates and evaluate their efficacy, pharmaceutical corporations use data mining.

4. Banking and Finance:

- **Credit Scoring**: By examining past financial information and credit histories, banks employ data mining to determine a customer's creditworthiness.

- **Fraud Detection**: Data mining identifies unique patterns and abnormalities in financial data, which aids in the detection of fraudulent transactions.

5. Production and quality assurance:

- **Process Optimization**: To optimize quality, lower defects, and increase productivity, data mining is used for industrial processes.

- **Predictive Maintenance**: Businesses may anticipate when equipment will break and plan maintenance by studying sensor data.

6. Logistics and Transportation:

- **Route Optimization:** Data mining is utilized to improve transportation routes, lowering costs and delivery times.

- **Inventory Management**: Businesses may utilize data mining to efficiently monitor inventory levels and cut storage expenses.

7. Social Media and Sentiment Analysis:

- **Sentiment Analysis**: Social media data is mined for sentiment data to determine how people feel about certain businesses, goods, or political topics.

- **Targeted Advertising**: Social media sites utilize data mining to provide people with targeted adverts based on their interests and actions.

8. Utility and energy:

- **Smart Grid Management**: Data mining enables utilities to forecast power outages and manage energy distribution.

- **Energy Consumption Analysis**: This technique is used to examine patterns of energy use and advise consumers on energy-saving actions.

9. Education:

- **Student Performance Analysis**: Data mining may assist educators in creating individualized lesson plans by identifying characteristics that affect student achievement.

- **Course Recommendations**: Based on students' academic records, educational institutions employ data mining to offer courses and resources to them.

10. **Environmental Science**:

- **Climate Modeling**: Climate data are mined using data mining techniques to forecast climate patterns, monitor environmental changes, and guide policymaking.

Data mining as a process:

Data scientists, analysts, and researchers utilize the data mining process as a systematic method to glean important patterns, trends, and insights from huge databases. It entails several sequential processes, each of which advances the overarching objective of deriving meaningful knowledge from data.

Common data mining techniques:

1. **Problem Definition**: The procedure starts with a precise comprehension of the issue or goal. What information or insight are you looking for from the data to try to answer a question? The problem's definition aids in directing data mining as a whole.

2. **Data Collection**: You obtain pertinent data from numerous sources in this stage. Both organized and unstructured data types, such as text, photos, and videos, may be found in databases and spreadsheets. The success of the analysis depends heavily on the calibre and volume of the data gathered.

3. **Data Preprocessing and Cleaning**: Raw data is frequently unorganized and contains mistakes, missing numbers, or inconsistent information. Data cleaning entails tasks including addressing missing data, getting rid of duplicates, and fixing mistakes. Preparing data for analysis also involves formatting it appropriately, for as by normalizing or scaling.

4. **Exploratory Data Analysis (EDA)**: EDA is the process of quantitatively and graphically investigating the data to understand its features and generate new insights. Common EDA approaches include data visualization tools, summary statistics, and data distribution analysis. EDA makes it easier to spot trends and anomalies that might aid with further investigation.

5. **Feature Selection and Engineering:** The analysis may not apply to all features (variables) in your dataset. While feature engineering may entail developing new features or modifying existing ones to enhance model performance, feature selection entails selecting the most crucial variables.

6. **Data Splitting**: A training set and a testing set are often created from the dataset. The testing set is used to assess the data mining model's performance once it has been built and trained.

The fundamental step in data mining is model building. Depending on the sort of problem you're trying to solve (classification, regression, clustering, etc.), you choose the right data mining method or machine learning approach. The model is then trained using the training set of data.

8. **Model Evaluation**: Using the testing data, you assess the model's performance once it has been trained. Depending on the particular issue, common assessment criteria include accuracy, precision, recall, F1-score, and others.

9. **Fine-tuning the model**: If the model's performance is subpar, you might need to tweak it by changing hyperparameters or experimenting with various techniques. Multiple iterations may be necessary for this stage.

10. **Deployment:** After creating a model that meets your needs, you put it into use. This can entail incorporating information into a corporate procedure, developing a software program, or utilizing it to inform decisions.

11. **Monitoring and Upkeep**: To guarantee that data mining models continue to function properly, they must be continuously monitored.

Model upgrades or retraining may be necessary due to changes in data trends over time.

12. **Documentation and Reporting**: It's crucial to keep track of your methods, conclusions, and insights throughout the process. For future reference and information exchange, clear documentation is helpful.

2

Chapter 2: Data Collection and Preparation

Sources and Types of Data:

Data sources are the sites or origins from where you acquire your data. You may get information for data mining from a variety of sources, such as:

1. **Databases**: These are data repositories that are structured. Data warehouses, relational databases, and NoSQL databases are frequently used as sources of structured data for data mining. Businesses and organizations frequently utilize databases to store transactional and historical data.

2. **Textual Materials**: Textual information from publications, reports, social media, emails, and other sources can be useful for text mining and NLP activities. These sources are semi- or unstructuredly organized.

3. **Web Information**: online crawling techniques may be used to scrape or gather data from websites and online services. Information from online forums, e-commerce websites, and other sources may be included in this data.

4. **Sensor Information:** Sensors gather information from numerous objects and settings for the Internet of Things (IoT). GPS locations, temperature measurements, and other information are examples of this data.

5. **Log Files**: Information regarding user activity, faults, and system performance may be found in server logs, application logs, and system logs. System optimization and troubleshooting can both benefit from log data analysis.

6. **Questionnaires & Surveys**: Structured data on a variety of subjects, such as consumer preferences, employee satisfaction, or market research, can be obtained using survey and questionnaire data.

7. **Govt. and Open Data:** Open data sets are made available by many government agencies and organizations on a variety of subjects, such as public health, economics, and demography. For study and analysis, these datasets are often utilized.

Types of Data:

Based on its structure and substance, data may be divided into several kinds. For data mining, it is crucial to comprehend the following data types:

1. **Structured data includes:** Structured data adheres to a predetermined format and is highly ordered. It is frequently included in relational databases and is simple to query using SQL. Examples include inventory data, sales transactions, and customer information tables.

2. **Unstructured Data:** Unstructured data is not tabularly arranged and has a specified structure. Text documents, pictures, audio files, and video files are some examples. Natural language processing (NLP) or image and speech recognition algorithms are frequently needed for unstructured data analysis.

3. **Semi-structured data:** Data that is semi-structured is arranged in parts and may have a flexible schema. It frequently has tags or metadata that give it some structure. XML files, JSON data, and HTML pages are a few examples.

4. **Temporal Data:** Because temporal data has a time component, it may be used in time series analysis. Weather information, event records, and stock price history are a few examples.

5. **Categorical Data:** Categorical data is made up of distinct groups or labels, including types of goods, clientele, or names of cities. It frequently occurs in categorization jobs.

6. **Numerical Information**: Continuous or discontinuous numerical quantities make up numerical data. Measurements like temperature, age, or wealth are a few examples. In tasks like grouping and regression, numerical data is frequently employed.

7. **Binary Information**: Only two potential values, generally 0 and 1, are available for binary data. It frequently serves as a symbol for on/off, true/false, and yes/no situations.

8. **Geographical Information:** Information related to geographic places, such as GPS coordinates, maps, and spatial connections, is included in geospatial data. It is utilized in location-based analysis and geographic information systems (GIS).

Data Collection Methods:

The strategies or procedures used to collect data from diverse sources for analysis, study, or decision-making are known as data-collecting methods. The type of data required, the goals of the research, the resources at hand, and the particular environment of the project all influence the choice of data-gathering technique. Here are a few typical techniques for gathering data:

1. Surveys and questionnaires, to start:

- In surveys, a predetermined set of questions is posed to a sample of respondents.

- Questionnaires can be distributed in person, via phone, email, or online forms.

- Surveys and questionnaires are appropriate for gathering organized facts and views from a broad population.

2. Interviews

- Direct interactions between an interviewer and a respondent take place during interviews.

- They might be open-ended or organized, containing questions that have been set.

- Interviews help acquire comprehensive data, decipher replies, and delve into complicated subjects.

3. Observation:

- Collecting data by observation entails observing and documenting actions, occurrences, or processes.

- It can be carried out in a controlled environment (such as a lab) or a natural setting (such as during ethnographic fieldwork).

- Observation is useful for understanding how people behave, interact, and experience occurrences.

4. **Document analysis comprises** looking at already-existing records, papers, and artefacts.

Historical records, reports, scholarly articles, and social media information are a few examples.

- This technique helps glean facts, patterns, and ideas from already-existing sources.

5. **Experimental Research**:

- To investigate cause-and-effect linkages, experimental research includes modifying variables in a regulated setting.

- It is frequently employed in scientific research to evaluate the effectiveness of certain interventions and test theories.

6. **Web scraping** entails the extraction of data from web pages and other online sources.

- Large volumes of organized or unstructured data are frequently gathered from the internet using this method.

- For this aim, web scraping tools and computer languages like Python are frequently employed.

7. **Sensor Data**: Sensors, like the ones used in Internet of Things (IoT) devices, may gather information on physical factors like temperature, humidity, and motion.

- Applications like environmental monitoring and industrial automation depend on sensor data.

8. **Focus groups**: Focus groups are frequently used to examine attitudes, perceptions, and views on a certain issue. They entail a led conversation among a small number of participants.

9. **Secondary data sources:** Secondary data is information that has been gathered by another party for a different objective.

- Publicly accessible datasets, official documents, or information from prior studies are all accessible to researchers.

- Although it can need thorough data validation and cleansing, this strategy can save time and money.

10. **Sampling Techniques**: Sampling techniques entail choosing a portion (a sample) of a larger population to collect data.

- To make sure the sample represents the target population, typical procedures include convenience sampling, random sampling, and stratified sampling.

Data Preprocessing and Cleaning:

Important elements in the data mining process include preprocessing and data cleansing. They entail changing the raw data into an appropriate format for modelling and preparing the data for analysis by locating and fixing mistakes, inconsistencies, and missing information. The accuracy and efficiency of data mining algorithms are highly impacted by the quality of the data, hence proper data cleaning and preprocessing are crucial. Here is a thorough breakdown of these two steps:

Data cleaning is step one:

The goal of data cleaning is to find and fix flaws and discrepancies in the dataset. It seeks to guarantee the reliability and accuracy of the data. Data cleansing routines often involve:

- **Taking Care of Missing Data**: Missing data may result in skewed findings or insufficient analysis. Imputation, which involves deleting records with missing values, utilizing specific markers for missing values, and deletion records with missing values are all ways to address missing data.

- **How to Deal with Outliers**: Data points known as outliers differ dramatically from the rest of the data. Modelling and statistical analysis may be distorted by them. Outliers can be dealt with in several ways, including removal, data transformation, and the use of powerful statistical tools.

- **Noise mitigation Data mistakes or random changes:** are referred to as noise. Especially with sensor data or data gathered from the actual world, techniques like smoothing and filtering can assist in decreasing noise.

Validation of Data comparing data with established guidelines or restrictions to find discrepancies. Assuring that age numbers are within a suitable range or that ZIP codes are accurate, for instance.

- **Data deduplication**: Eliminating redundant records from the dataset by locating them and eliminating them.

- **Data standardization**: Putting data into a dependable format. For instance, normalizing text data (such as changing text to lowercase) or converting units of measurement. Another example would be translating dates into a standard date format.

Data Preprocessing:

Data preprocessing entails converting cleansed data into a format appropriate for modelling and analysis. This stage guarantees that algorithms can successfully extract patterns and insights from the data and prepare it for them. Typical data preparation activities consist of:

- **Normalization and Scaling:** Scaling numerical characteristics to a common range (for example, between 0 and 1) to avoid bigger magnitude features from predominating the model.

- **Categorical Variables Encoding**: transforming categorical information into numerical form, such as gender and city. Techniques like label encoding and one-hot encoding can be used for this.

- **Feature Selection**: To minimize dimensionality and enhance model performance, identify and choose the important features while eliminating the redundant or unnecessary ones.

Text Data Processing Tokenization, stemming, and the removal of stop words (frequent words like "and" or "the" that may not contribute value), among other activities, may be applied to natural language data.

Dealing with Unbalanced Data Techniques like oversampling, undersampling, or creating synthetic data can be used to balance the classes in datasets with unbalanced classes (where one class considerably outnumbers the others).

- Resampling, managing time-related features, and feature engineering are crucial elements in the time-series preprocessing process.

How to Handle Missing Data:

Since incomplete or missing values frequently appear in real-world datasets, dealing with missing data is an essential stage in the data mining process. Inaccurate or biased outcomes in data analysis and modelling might result from improper handling of missing data.

Here are some typical approaches and things to think about when dealing with missing data:

1. **Recognizing Missing Data**: - It's crucial to determine which values in your dataset are missing before taking any action about missing data. To find missing numbers, you might make use of software tools, summary statistics, or data visualization.

2. **Recognizing the Sources of Missing Data:** Missing data can happen for several reasons, such as incorrect data input, incomplete data collection, or purposeful omission of data. Choosing the best handling approach may be aided by knowing the causes.

3. **Data Imputation**: Imputation includes substituting estimated or anticipated values for missing values. Typical imputation techniques include:

   - **Mean/Median/Mode Imputation:** Substitute missing values in the same column with their mean, median, or mode. This is straightforward but might not be appropriate if the data is not evenly distributed.

   - **Regression Imputation:** Regression models may be used to forecast missing values by looking at how they relate to other variables.

   - **K-Nearest Neighbors (K-NN) Imputation**: In a multidimensional space, replace missing values with values from the K-nearest data points.

   - **Interpolation**: Estimate missing values based on nearby data points using interpolation techniques (linear, cubic, etc.).

- **Machine Learning Imputation**: Develop machine learning models that can forecast missing values based on the information that is already available.

4. Deletion of Missing Data:

- In some circumstances, it could be necessary to eliminate rows or columns that have missing data. Listwise or pairwise deletion is the term used for this.

- Remove all rows with missing values using the listwise deletion method. This may result in a large loss of data.

- **Pairwise Deletion**: Examine the available data for each analysis, omitting any variables with missing values.

5. Generate Missing Data Indicators:

- You may generate binary indicators (flags) for missing values in each column as opposed to imputing or removing them. You may then take missing data into account when doing your analysis.

6. Domain-specific expertise: Having this expertise can sometimes help you decide how to handle missing data. For instance, you could approach missing data differently if certain situations are more likely to result in them.

7. Multiple Imputation:

- Using multiple imputations, missing data are imputed many times to take uncertainty into account. To get more precise estimates and confidence ranges, it entails the creation of numerous datasets with various imputed values.

8. **Take into Account the Impact on Analysis**: Always think about the potential effects on your analysis or modelling of the chosen strategy for managing missing data. In research or reporting, it's critical to be open and honest about your methodology.

9. **Sensitivity Analysis:**

- Assess the sensitivity of your findings to various approaches to addressing missing data. This makes it easier to evaluate how solid your findings are.

10. **Documentation**:

- Keep thorough records of your procedures for handling missing data, as these documents are crucial for replication and openness in research.

3

Chapter 3: Exploratory Data Analysis (EDA)

Overview of EDA:

A basic grasp of this important stage in the data analysis process is provided through an overview of exploratory data analysis (EDA). Before using more sophisticated statistical or machine learning methods, data scientists and analysts first evaluate and summarize large data sets to find trends, spot outliers, and obtain insights. These are EDA's main components:

1. **EDA's**: primary goal is to comprehend a data set's structure, traits, and distinguishing qualities. It aids in the creation of hypotheses and the discovery of preliminary patterns, which can direct further data analysis and modelling.

2. **Data Visualization**: EDA frequently entails the production of several visuals, such as density plots, box plots, scatter plots, and histograms.

- Data distribution, the connections between variables, and the occurrence of outliers are all investigated using visualizations.

3. **Summary Statistics**: EDA computes summary statistics like mean, median, mode, variance, and standard deviation. These statistics offer a summary of the data's primary patterns and variability.

4. **Identifying and evaluating** missing data within the dataset is done using EDA.

- At this step, choices on how to handle missing data, such as imputation or removal, may be made.

5. **Outlier Detection**: Outliers are data points that differ noticeably from the dataset's regular trend.

- Outliers can significantly affect future studies, therefore EDA seeks to find and look into them.

6. **Pattern Recognition**: EDA entails examining the data for patterns and trends. This may involve locating clusters in multidimensional data, seasonality in time-series data, or relationships between variables.

7. **Data Transformation**: EDA may occasionally require data transformation to improve its suitability for analysis.

   - Log transformations, normalization, and standardization are often used transformations.

8. **Interactive Exploration**:

   - Analysts iteratively explore the data during EDA, which is frequently an interactive process.

   - Analysts may apply filters or subsets to the data, focus on particular features, or do drill-down analysis.

9. **Hypothesis Generation**: EDA may inspire the creation of theories about connections or patterns in the data. Later on in the investigation, these assumptions can be verified.

10. **Communication of Insights**: EDA results are frequently shared via reports, presentations, or visual dashboards.

   - It is crucial for decision-makers to comprehend the consequences of insights through effective communication.

Techniques for data visualization:

Data mining and analysis depend heavily on data visualization. To better enable consumers to comprehend patterns, trends, and insights within the data, it entails visually portraying the data. The following is a description of several popular data visualization methods:

1. Bar Charts:

- Rectangular bars are used in bar charts to depict categorical data.

- They are great for contrasting the sizes of various groups.

- They come in both horizontal and vertical varieties (horizontal bar chart).

2. Histograms: are used to display the distribution of continuous or discrete data. They divide the data into intervals or bins and show the frequency or density of the data points inside each interval or bin.

3. Line charts: are used to show data points connected by lines.

- They are frequently applied to time series data to demonstrate recurring patterns and trends.

4. Scatter Plots: Individual data points are shown as dots on a two-dimensional plane in scatter plots. They help illustrate connections between two continuous variables, such as clustering or correlation.

5. Pie charts: Pie charts show pieces of a whole, with each category representing a piece of the pie.

- They can be used to show a dataset's structure, but they should be used with caution because they may not be as useful as bar charts for comparing values.

6. **Heatmaps:** Heatmaps make use of colours to show how big values are in a matrix or grid. They are frequently used to show correlation matrices, geographic information, and clustering outcomes.

7. **Box Plots (Box-and-Whisker Plots):** Box plots offer a graphic description of the data distribution.

- They make it simple to detect skewness or variability in a dataset by displaying the median, quartiles, and probable outliers.

8. **Bubble Charts:**

- Similar to scatter plots, bubble charts also have a third variable, which is represented by the size of the data points (bubbles).

- They help create three-dimensional data visualizations.

9. **Treemaps**: Treemaps provide hierarchical information as layered rectangles. The hierarchical structure of a dataset, such as file directories or organizational hierarchies, is frequently shown using them.

10. **Choropleth maps**: These maps show data values by geographic areas using colours or shading.

- They are frequently used to represent local statistics, such as income levels, population density, or election results.

11. **Word clouds**: Word clouds highlight terms in a text collection graphically according to their frequency or significance.

- They can highlight important phrases or topics in a manuscript and are frequently used for text analysis.

12. **Network Diagrams**:

- Network diagrams use nodes and edges to depict relationships between items.

- They help display intricate data linkages, including social or transportation networks.

Summary Statistics:

Descriptive statistics are numerical measurements that offer a succinct summary of a dataset's key features. Summary statistics fall under this category. Without having to look at each data point separately, these statistics assist analysts and data scientists in distilling and comprehending a dataset's key characteristics. To quickly get insights into your data, summary statistics are an essential component of data analysis and are essential to data mining. Here are some typical summaries of the data:

1. **Measures of the central tendency are as follows**: By adding up each value in the dataset and dividing by the total number of data points, the mean is obtained. It indicates the data's "average" value.

- **Median:** When the values are ordered, the median is the middle value in the dataset. It measures the middle location and is unaffected by extreme values.

2. **Measures of Dispersion:**

- **Variance**: Variance calculates the degree of deviation between the data points and the mean. The average of the squared deviations between each data point and the mean is calculated.

- **Standard Deviation**: The variance's square root yields the standard deviation. It gives a measurement of the data's dispersion or spread.

3. **Distribution shape measurements include skewness.** The asymmetry of the data distribution is measured by skewness. A positive skew suggests a rightward skew (tail on the right), whereas a negative skew indicates a leftward skew.

- **Kurtosis:** This statistic assesses the "tailedness" of the data distribution. Low kurtosis denotes light tails, whereas high kurtosis denotes hefty tails.

4. **Quantiles and Percentiles**: The data is divided into 100 equal pieces using percentiles. The data value below which 25% of the data falls, for instance, is the 25th percentile.

- **Quartiles:** The data is divided into four equal sections using quartiles. The median is represented by the second quartile (Q2), the 75th percentile is represented by the third quartile (Q3), and the first quartile (Q1) is the 25th percentile.

5. **Range**: The range represents the discrepancy between the dataset's highest and minimum values. It offers a straightforward measurement of the data's dispersion.

6. **IQR (Interquartile Range)**: The interval between the first and third quartiles is known as the IQR. In comparison to the complete range, it reflects the middle 50% of the data and is less susceptible to outliers.

7. **Summary graphs and tables:** In addition to numerical statistics, summary statistics can also contain tables and graphs that graphically depict the properties of the data, such as histograms, box plots, and frequency distributions.

Software and EDA Tools:

Data analysts and data scientists need exploratory data analysis (EDA) tools and software to explore and visualize data, obtain insights, and make defensible conclusions. Before using more sophisticated data mining or machine learning approaches, EDA is essential for comprehending the underlying patterns, correlations, and properties of a dataset. Here is a description of EDA software and tools:

1. **Spreadsheet applications**, such as Google Sheets and Microsoft Excel

These frequently used tools offer fundamental data processing and visualization skills.

- To study data, users may construct charts, histograms, scatter plots, and summary statistics.

- Appropriate for small to medium-sized datasets and fundamental EDA tasks.

2. **Python Data Science Libraries (such as Seaborn, Pandas, NumPy, and Matplotlib):**

Python is a well-known programming language for data analysis and has strong EDA modules.

- Pandas are used for basic analysis, data cleaning, and modification.

- A variety of visualizations are made using Matplotlib and Seaborn.

- NumPy offers support for mathematical functions and numerical computations.

3. **R Programming Language**: R is an advanced language for data analysis and statistics that offers a wide range of EDA-related tools.

- For data visualization and manipulation, packages like ggplot2, dplyr, and tidyr are frequently used.

- R's interactive interface is ideal for interactive data exploration.

4. **Jupyter Notebooks**: Users may blend code, graphics, and explanatory text in Jupyter Notebooks, an interactive online environment.

- Since you can execute code cells to carry out analytical stages and instantly observe the results, they are well-liked for use in EDA.

5. **Tableau**: Tableau is an effective tool for data visualization that enables users to build dynamic and interactive dashboards.

- It can execute EDA by drag-and-drop operations and link to different data sources.

- Appropriate for both simple and complex EDA operations.

6. Another well-liked business intelligence tool for data visualization and analysis is **Microsoft's Power BI**. Through data exploration and visualization, it helps EDA and offers interactive dashboards.

7. **Statistical software (such as SAS and SPSS)**: In research and corporate environments, these specialist software programs are frequently used for sophisticated statistical analysis and EDA. They provide a huge selection of statistical analyses and alternatives for data display.

8. **Data mining software, like RapidMiner and KNIME.**

These systems were created for end-to-end data mining, which starts with EDA.

- They handle a variety of data preparation and analysis operations and provide a visual workflow interface.

9. **Open-Source Data Visualization Libraries (like Plotly and Bokeh)**: These libraries enable web-based and interactive data visualization.

- To study data, users may make interactive graphs and dashboards.

4

Chapter 4: Data Mining Techniques

Supervised Learning:

A key idea in machine learning and data mining is supervised learning. It describes a type of machine learning in which the algorithm picks up new information from a labelled dataset, which implies that the training data contains both the input characteristics and the associated right output or target values. The main objective of supervised learning is to discover a mapping or function that, using the patterns discovered from the labelled instances, can forecast the results for novel, unseen data.

The two primary supervised learning tasks are:

1. Classification:

- The objective of classification is to categorize or classify data items. These classes can stand in for a variety of categories or labels, including positive, negative, or neutral sentiment, spam, disease, or no disease.

- Classification algorithms can forecast the class membership of fresh data points by learning decision boundaries in the feature space that demarcates various classes.

2. Regression:

On the other hand, regression is used to forecast a real number or a continuous numerical value. It is frequently used for estimating or forecasting a given quantity, such as when estimating property prices based on factors like square footage, the number of bedrooms, and location.

Regression algorithms often fit a curve or a surface to the data to represent the connection between the input characteristics and the target variable.

<u>Classification</u>:

A special goal in supervised learning is classification, in which the computer learns to group incoming data into predetermined groups or labels. Key ideas about categorization are as follows:

A classification algorithm would aim to examine the properties of these emails and identify which category (spam or not spam) each new, unlabeled email belongs to. - **Example**: Suppose you have a dataset of emails, and each email is labelled as either "spam" or "not spam."

Types of Classification techniques:

Several techniques may be used to classify data, including decision trees, logistic regression, k-nearest neighbours (K-NN), support vector machines (SVM), and neural networks.

- **Evaluation Metrics**: Classification algorithms are evaluated using matrices for confusion, recall, accuracy, precision, and F1-score. These metrics aid in gauging how well the algorithm classifies data points.

- **Applications:** Classification is frequently used in fraud detection, sentiment analysis, tumour identification, image recognition, and medical diagnostics (such as spam email detection).

<u>Regression</u>:

Another important job in supervised learning is regression, which is mostly used to forecast continuous numerical values. Regression's main points are as follows:

- **Example**: Take into account a dataset that contains details on homes, such as their size, number of bedrooms, and location, as well as their sale prices. An algorithm for regression seeks to develop a model that can foretell the sale price of a new home based on the property's attributes.

- **Linear regression**, polynomial regression, ridge regression, support vector regression, and other popular regression algorithms are examples of the several types of regression algorithms.

- **Evaluation Metrics**: Metrics that determine how well a regression model's predictions match the actual data include mean squared error (MSE), root mean squared error (RMSE), mean absolute error (MAE), and R-squared (R2).

- **Applications**: Regression is used in a wide range of fields, including finance to anticipate stock prices, economics to predict trends, healthcare to estimate patient outcomes, and engineering to monitor quality.

Unsupervised Learning:

Unsupervised learning algorithms are trained on data without any direct supervision. In other words, without being given labelled results or categories, the algorithm searches for patterns, structures, or correlations in the data. Clustering and association rule mining are two frequently used approaches in unsupervised learning.

Clustering:

Unsupervised learning techniques such as clustering entail assembling related data points into clusters or segments based on their intrinsic commonalities. Finding hidden patterns and structures in the data without any prior awareness of those patterns is the main objective of clustering. The following are some essential clustering points:

- **Objective**: The main goal of clustering is to divide up a dataset into groups in which the data points are more similar to one another than to those in other groups.

- **Applications**: Clustering is used in a broad variety of fields, such as marketing, natural language processing, image segmentation, and computer vision.

- There are several clustering techniques, including Gaussian Mixture Models (GMM), Density-Based Spatial Clustering of

Applications with Noise (DBSCAN), Hierarchical Clustering, and K-Means. To define clusters based on distance, density, or probabilistic models, each program takes a different technique.

- **assessment:** Cluster assessment tools like the Davies-Bouldin index and silhouette score are used to rate the accuracy of clustering outcomes.

Mining Association Rules:

Another unsupervised learning method that focuses on finding intriguing connections or links between variables in huge datasets is association rule mining. It is very helpful for identifying trends in databases or transactional data. A few essential ideas concerning association rule mining are as follows:

Finding rules that show statistical connections between objects or characteristics in a dataset is the main goal of association rule mining. These laws are frequently stated as "If X, then Y."

- **Applications**: Association rule mining is frequently used in fraud detection (e.g., spotting odd patterns in transactions), recommendation systems (e.g., suggesting products or content based on user behaviour), and market basket analysis (e.g., identifying items frequently bought together in a grocery store).

- **Algorithms**: For association rule mining, the Apriori algorithm is a well-known and often employed approach. It recognizes common itemsets and builds association rules from them.

- **Metrics**: Association rule mining frequently uses metrics like support, confidence, and lift to assess the robustness and allure of rules that are found.

Semi-Supervised Learning:

A kind of machine learning called semi-supervised learning combines aspects of supervised learning and unsupervised learning. You have a dataset for semi-supervised learning that includes both labelled and unlabeled data points. This method allows you to train machine learning models using a smaller quantity of labelled data in combination with a bigger pool of unlabeled data, which is especially helpful when gathering labelled data is expensive or time-consuming.

The following are significant factors to think about while using semi-supervised learning:

1. Compared to unlabeled data:

- **Labeled Data**: This subset of the dataset consists of data points where every instance has been explicitly marked with the appropriate output or target label. Each data point has a class label attached to it in the categorization context.

- **Unlabeled Data:** Explicit target labels are absent from unlabeled data points. These data points are frequently plentiful and could be less expensive to gather than labelled data.

2. What Happens During Semi-Supervised Learning?

- Semi-supervised learning techniques seek to improve prediction models by making use of the information included in both labelled and unlabeled data.

- To increase model accuracy utilizing the unlabeled data, the algorithms in semi-supervised learning may employ self-training, co-training, or other techniques.

3. Benefits of semi-supervised learning include:

- **Cost-Efficiency**: By complementing the few labelled data with a wealth of unlabeled data, you may maximize its use while saving money and time on labelling.

- **Improved Generalization**: Semi-supervised learning models frequently generalize better and have the potential to attain higher accuracy as a result of using more data.

- **Real-World Applicability**: Acquiring large volumes of labelled data might be difficult in many real-world circumstances, making semi-supervised learning a viable option.

4. Challenges and Things to Think About

- **Quality of Labels**: The effectiveness of semi-supervised learning is strongly influenced by the correctness of the labelled data. Model mistakes may result from inaccurate or noisy labelling.

Semi-supervised algorithms frequently use the assumption that the distribution of unlabeled data is comparable to that of the labelled data, however, this is not always the case.

- **Selection Bias:** If bias is introduced during the collection of labelled data, it may have an impact on the model's performance.

5. Cases for Use:

- Semi-supervised learning is used in a variety of industries, including audio processing, picture identification, and natural language processing (such as text categorization).

- When there is a lack of labelled medical data, it might be utilized in healthcare for illness diagnosis.

In recommendation systems, when user preferences may be partially labelled, it is also useful.

6. Techniques and Algorithms:

- Some well-known semi-supervised learning techniques include label propagation, multi-view learning, self-training, and co-training.

- In semi-supervised situations, deep learning approaches, such as self-supervised pre-training followed by fine-tuning with labelled data, have proved effective.

Reinforcement Learning:

A form of machine learning called reinforcement learning (RL) teaches an agent to make a series of decisions by interacting with its surroundings. It draws on behavioural psychology, where learning is motivated by trial and error to accomplish certain objectives. By getting feedback in the form of incentives or penalties depending on their behaviour, reinforcement learning (RL) algorithms allow agents to learn the best methods or policies.

defining characteristics of reinforcement learning:

1. The learner or decision-maker who engages with the environment is an agent. The agent acts to maximize its long-term cumulative benefits.

2. The external system that the agent communicates with is known as the environment. The environment responds to the agent's activities by giving it feedback. Anything from a video game to a robotic device may be it.

3. A representation of the environment's current state or configuration is referred to as a state (s). The environment in which an agent makes decisions is defined by states. States can sometimes be seen clearly, while other times they may need to be inferred.

4. The range of actions or decisions an agent may make in a certain condition is referred to as action (a). The agent decides the actions to take in order to change states.

5. A policy is a plan of action or set of guidelines that an agent uses to determine what to do in different situations. The policy may be stochastic or deterministic.

6. An environmental signal that is given as a reward (r) for each activity. The payment represents the immediate gain or loss resulting from the agent's conduct. To maximize the cumulative reward over time is the agent's objective.

7. **Value Function (V)**: A function that calculates the anticipated total gain that an agent can expect from a specific state or state-action pair. It aids the agent in determining if various conditions or deeds are desirable.

8. The Q-function (Q) predicts the predicted cumulative reward explicitly for state-action pairings, much like the value function does. Algorithms for Q-learning frequently employ it.

Algorithms for reinforcement learning are created to determine the best course of action that maximizes the predicted long-term reward. Several popular reinforcement learning algorithms are as follows:

- **Q-Learning**: An off-policy technique that uses iterative updates based on the Bellman equation to discover the best action-value function (Q-function).

- **Deep Q-Networks (DQN)**: This deep learning-based strategy combines Q-learning with neural networks, making it appropriate for high-dimensional state spaces.

- **Policy Gradient Methods**: These techniques directly improve the policy to increase anticipated benefits. This group includes algorithms like Proximal Policy Optimization (PPO) and REINFORCE.

- **Actor-Critic Methods**: These techniques pair policy optimization (the actor) with value estimate (the critic). This method is used by algorithms like Advantage Actor-Critic (A2C) and Advantage-Weighted Actor-Critic (A3C).

Anomaly Detection:

A data mining approach called anomaly detection, often referred to as outlier identification, is used to find patterns or data points in a dataset that significantly depart from the norm. These anomalies are rare, odd, or unexpected findings that may contain important information or point to possible issues. Many industries, including banking, cybersecurity, industrial quality control, and healthcare, among others, employ anomaly detection extensively.

The following are some essential features and elements of anomaly detection:

1. Various Anomalies:

- **Point Anomalies**: These are specific instances of data that deviate dramatically from the rest of the data. For instance, a point anomaly in the detection of credit card fraud may be an extremely high transaction amount.

- **Contextual Anomalies**: When identifying anomalies, one must take into account the environment in which the data point occurs. An example of a contextual anomaly would be a sudden increase in website traffic that occurs outside of regular business hours.

- **Collective Anomalies**: These anomalies concern a collection of connected data points that, when taken as a whole, reveal strange behaviour. An illustration might be a pattern of exceptionally high CPU use across several servers in a data centre.

2. Techniques for Detecting Anomalies:

- **Statistical approaches**: These approaches entail finding data points that deviate greatly from the predicted values and modelling the statistical features of the data, such as mean, variance, or distribution.

- **K-nearest neighbours** (KNN), isolation forests, and one-class SVM (Support Vector Machines) are a few examples of supervised and unsupervised machine learning techniques that may be utilized for anomaly identification.

- **Deep Learning**: Deep neural networks, in particular autoencoders, can recognize abnormalities in high-dimensional data and learn complicated patterns.

- **Time Series Analysis**: Time series data-specific anomaly detection methods, such as ARIMA (AutoRegressive Integrated Moving Average) or Exponential Smoothing, are utilized for tasks like spotting equipment malfunctions and stock market abnormalities.

3. Metrics for evaluation:

- The Receiver Operating Characteristic (ROC) curve, precision, recall, and F1-score are common metrics for assessing anomaly detection algorithms. These measures aid in evaluating the model's accuracy in spotting abnormalities while reducing false positives.

4. Applications:

- There are many uses for anomaly detection, including seeing fraud in financial transactions, spotting network intrusions in cybersecurity, spotting manufacturing defects, spotting uncommon diseases in healthcare, and monitoring equipment health.

5. Challenges:

- Due to skewed datasets, where anomalies are uncommon relative to typical data points, anomaly identification can be difficult. It can be challenging to interpret models, particularly when using deep learning techniques.

6. Considerations:

- The type of predicted anomalies, the nature of the data, and the particular application all influence the anomaly detection technique selection. The detection rate and the false positive rate are frequently trade-offs.

5

Chapter 5: Data Mining Algorithms

Decision Trees:

Decision trees are a well-known machine learning and data mining approach that may be utilized for classification and regression applications. They are a flexible decision-making tool that is especially useful for novices owing to their intuitive nature. The following is an explanation of decision trees:

1. What exactly is a Decision Tree?

A decision tree is a graphical depiction of a decision-making process or a mapping from observations about a particular object to inferences about its goal value. It resembles an upside-down tree, with each node representing a choice or a test on an attribute, each branch representing a decision outcome, and each leaf node representing a class label or a goal value.

2. What Is the Process of Using a Decision Tree?

The following steps are involved in the development of a decision tree:

a. **Root Node**: Select the best characteristic from the dataset to serve as the tree's root. This feature is chosen based on factors such as information gain, Gini impurity, and entropy. The most significant characteristic of the classification or regression job is the root node.

b. Divide the dataset into subgroups based on the values of the selected attribute. Each subset represents a branch from the root node to a child node.

c. **Child Nodes**: Repeat the procedure of picking the best attribute from the subset of data associated with that node for each child node. This recursive procedure will continue until one of the halting requirements is fulfilled.

d. Stopping requirements for leaf nodes may include reaching a maximum depth, having a minimum number of samples in a node, or obtaining homogeneity in goal values. When a stopping condition is satisfied, a leaf node with a class label (in classification) or a predicted value (in regression) is formed.

3. Algorithms for Decision Trees:

There are various decision tree algorithms, the most common of which are:

- **CART (Classification and Regression Trees)**: CART is a flexible method that may be used for classification as well as regression. It employs classification criteria such as Gini impurity and regression criteria such as mean squared error.

- **ID3 (Iterative Dichotomiser 3)**: ID3 is generally used for classification jobs and selects characteristics using the information gain criteria and entropy.

- **C4.5**: Like ID3, C4.5 works for classification and employs the gain ratio criteria and entropy.

- **Random Forests**: Random forests are an ensemble approach for improving accuracy and reducing overfitting by combining numerous decision trees.

4. Decision trees provide the following advantages:

- **Interpretability**: Because decision trees are simple to read and draw, they are useful for presenting the logic behind a choice.

- **Handling Non-Linearity**: They are capable of capturing complicated non-linear correlations in data without the need for sophisticated mathematical calculations.

- **Feature Importance**: Decision trees can tell you how important each feature is in a classification or regression operation.

5. Decision trees have the following limitations:

- **Overfitting**: Decision trees, especially deep and complicated ones, are prone to overfitting. Pruning or limiting tree depth can assist in alleviating this problem.

- **Instability**: Because small changes in data might result in various tree architectures, decision trees are somewhat unstable.

- **Bias Toward Dominant Classes**: Decision trees may prefer the dominant class in classification tasks with unbalanced datasets.

Naive Bayes:

Naive Bayes: is a straightforward yet effective classification technique that is frequently used in data mining, machine learning, and natural language processing. It is based on Bayes' theorem, a fundamental concept in probability theory, and is especially effective for text classification, spam detection, sentiment analysis, and a variety of other applications where data must be sorted into multiple categories or classes.

Here's a rundown of the Naive Bayes algorithm's essential principles and workings:

1. **Theorem of Bayes**:

- Bayes' theorem, which defines the likelihood of an occurrence based on previous knowledge of conditions that may be relevant to that event, lies at the heart of Naive Bayes. The following is the formula for Bayes' theorem:

$$P(A|B) = \frac{P(B|A) \cdot P(A)}{P(B)}$$

- In terms of categorisation, we have:

- A: The class label (the category to which the data should be assigned).

- B: The data's characteristics or properties.

2. **Foolish Assumption**:

- The "Naive" in Naive Bayes refers to a simplification assumption made by the algorithm. Given the class title, it assumes that all characteristics are conditionally independent. In other words, it assumes that once the class name is established, the presence or absence of one characteristic is independent of the presence or absence of any other feature.

3. **Classification**:

The Naive Bayes method evaluates the probability of a new data point belonging to each conceivable class given a new data point with a set of characteristics.

- It computes the conditional probability for each class using Bayes' theorem and the Naive assumption.

- As the projected class label, the class with the highest conditional probability is assigned to the data point.

4. **Naive Bayes Models**:

- There are several types of Naive Bayes classifiers, and the one to employ is determined by the nature of the data:

- **Multinomial Naive Bayes**: Suitable for discrete data, multinomial Naive Bayes is frequently used in text classification when features reflect word counts or frequencies.

- **Gaussian Naive Bayes**: This method is suitable for continuous data with a Gaussian (normal) distribution.

- **Bernoulli Naive Bayes**: Good for binary data with binary variables (e.g., 0s and 1s).

5. **Training**:

- Labeled data with known class labels is required to train a Naive Bayes classifier.

- The approach computes the prior probability ($P(A)$) and likelihood probabilities ($P(B|A)$) of the features given each class.

- These probabilities are used to forecast fresh, unlabeled data.

6. **Smoothing**:

- Smoothing techniques such as Laplace smoothing (add-one smoothing) are frequently used to prevent zero probability when a characteristic has not been seen in a certain class during training.

7. **Benefits and Drawbacks**:
  - **<u>Benefits</u>**:
  - Easy to use and computationally efficient.
  - Effective with high-dimensional data.
  - Outperforms many real-world applications, particularly text categorization.

- **<u>Restrictions</u>**:
  - Relies on the Naive assumption, which may not always be true.
  - Can be sensitive to irrelevant characteristics.
  - Accurate results need a substantial amount of training data.

K-Means Clustering:

K-means clustering is a common unsupervised machine-learning approach for grouping or clustering data. K-Means' main purpose is to partition a dataset into K clusters, with each data point belonging to the cluster with the closest mean value. It is frequently utilized in a variety of disciplines such as data analysis, picture processing, and client segmentation. Here's a detailed breakdown of how the K-Means algorithm works:

1. **Initialization**:
   - Determine the number of clusters to be created, K.
   - Choose K data points at random from the dataset to serve as the first cluster centroids. These are the first cluster representatives.

2. **Assignment**:
   - Calculate the distance between each data point in the dataset and each of the K centroids. Euclidean distance and Manhattan distance are two common distance measurements.
   - Assign each data point to the cluster with the nearest centroid. This is normally accomplished by picking the cluster with the shortest distance.

3. **Centroids Update**:
   - Recalculate the centroids of each cluster after allocating all data points to clusters. A cluster's centroid is the mean of all the data points in that cluster.
   - For each cluster, compute the updated centroids.

4. **Steps 2 and 3 should be repeated**:
   - Repeat the assignment and update processes until one of the halting conditions is satisfied. Stopping criteria that are commonly used include:

- **Convergence**: The algorithm has converged if the cluster assignments do not vary considerably between rounds.

- **A specified number of iterations**: You can choose a maximum number of iterations, after which the algorithm will terminate.

- **Centroid stability**: If the difference in centroids between iterations is less than a given threshold, the method is said to be converged.

5. Final Outcome:

- Your final clustering result is obtained when the algorithm converges or reaches the maximum number of repetitions.

- You know the coordinates of the K centroids and each data point corresponds to one of the K clusters.

Although K-Means is a simple and efficient method, it does have several restrictions and considerations:

- It assumes that clusters are spherical, uniform in size, and have identical densities, which may not necessarily be the case in real-world data.

- Because the algorithm's performance might be affected by the initial location of centroids, several initializations are frequently employed.

- Determining the appropriate number of clusters, K, can be subjective and needs domain expertise or assessment criteria such as the elbow approach.

- Because outliers can have a major impact on K-Means results, it is critical to preprocess data and perhaps apply outlier identification algorithms.

Apriori Algorithm:

The Apriori method is a well-known data mining tool for mining association rules in huge datasets. It is frequently used in a variety of applications, such as market basket analysis, recommendation systems, and others. The Apriori algorithm's primary purpose is to find frequent item sets and construct association rules based on these item sets. The Apriori algorithm is explained in detail below:

1. **Frequently Generated Itemsets**:

- The method begins by scanning the dataset for each item's (or item's) support (frequency). The number of transactions in which an item set occurs is its support.

- The technique begins by assuming that all individual items in the dataset are frequent itemsets.

2. **Pruning**:

- Apriori discovers common itemsets using a "bottom-up" technique. It leverages the Apriori property, which stipulates that if an item is rare, all of its supersets (bigger itemsets including it) must likewise be uncommon.

- To put this idea into practice, the algorithm creates bigger candidate itemsets by aggregating frequent itemsets discovered in the preceding iteration.

- Following the generation of candidate itemsets, it prunes those that are not possibly common based on the Apriori property, hence minimizing the search space.

3. Support Level:

- As an input parameter, the algorithm requires a minimum support threshold. Only itemsets with more than this amount of support are deemed frequent.

- The support threshold aids in the elimination of itemsets that occur much too seldom to be deemed relevant.

4. Iterations should be repeated:

- The procedure of creating candidate itemsets, pruning, and counting support is repeated until no more frequent itemsets can be identified or the necessary level of itemset size is attained.

- The output of this phase is a list of frequently occurring itemsets and their support numbers.

5. Association Rule Development:

- The Apriori algorithm builds association rules from common itemsets after detecting them.

- An association rule is a statement of the type "if A then B," where A and B are itemsets and the rule is formed from them.

- The method computes the confidence of each rule, which indicates the probability that itemset B will be purchased if itemset

A has been purchased. Confidence is determined as the sum of A and B's support divided by A's support.

- To filter out weak rules, the algorithm uses a user-defined minimum confidence level.

6. **Output**:

- The Apriori algorithm produces a set of association rules that fulfil the minimal support and confidence criteria.

Support Vector Machines (SVM):

SVMs are a sophisticated and flexible family of supervised machine-learning algorithms that may be utilized for both classification and regression applications. They are especially popular for handling complicated issues in computer vision, natural language processing, and bioinformatics. SVMs are well-known for their capacity to handle high-dimensional data and their resilience in the face of outliers. Here's an overview of SVMs and its essential concepts:

1. **Linear Separability**: The notion of linear separability serves as the foundation for SVMs. SVM tries to identify a hyperplane (a decision boundary) that optimally divides two classes of data points in binary classification. The goal is to locate the hyperplane with the

greatest margin, which is the distance between the hyperplane and the nearest data points in each class.

2. **SVMs are sometimes referred to as "maximum margin classifiers"** since they strive to maximize the margin between data points of various classes. Support vectors are the data points nearest to the decision border. These are the most essential data points since they define the hyperplane's position and orientation.

3. SVMs may handle non-linearly separable data by translating the input characteristics into a higher-dimensional space with the use of a mathematical function known as a kernel. Kernels that are commonly used include linear, polynomial, radial basis function (RBF), and sigmoid kernels. The kernel used is determined by the nature of the data and the situation at hand.

4. **Soft Margin**: In practice, data is frequently not fully separable, and there may be some overlap between classes or outliers. SVMs can deal with this by incorporating a soft margin. To establish a compromise between maximizing the margin and avoiding misclassification mistakes, the soft margin allows for some misclassification of data points. The trade-off between margin size and misclassification is regulated by the hyperparameter "C."

5. **Support Vector Classification**: SVMs are utilized for binary classification issues in support vector classification (SVC). The goal is to determine the best hyperplane between two classes while

maximizing the margin and compensating for misclassification inside the soft margin.

6. **Support Vector Regression**: SVMs may be used for regression problems as well. The purpose of support vector regression (SVR) is to identify a hyperplane that predicts a continuous target variable. Rather than maximizing the margin, SVR seeks to reduce data point departure from the hyperplane while allowing for a regulated level of error.

7. SVMs contain various hyperparameters that must be tweaked to attain optimal performance. In addition to the regularization parameter C and the kernel selection, additional hyperparameters, such as kernel-specific parameters, may need to be modified using techniques such as cross-validation.

8. **SVM Advantages**:
   - Useful in three-dimensional spaces.
   - Resistant to overfitting, especially when properly regularized.
   - Due to the usage of various kernels, it is versatile.
   - Appropriate for classification and regression workloads.
   - Effectively handles outliers.

9. **SVM limitations:**
   - Can be computationally costly, particularly when dealing with huge datasets.
   - Kernel selection can be difficult and may need domain expertise.

- The model's interpretability may be constrained, particularly with complicated kernels.

- Unsuitable for multi-class classification without enhancements such as one-vs-all.

Neural Networks:

A neural network is a computer model inspired by the structure and operation of the human brain. It is also known as an artificial neural network (ANN) or simply a neural net. Neural networks are a subset of machine learning and deep learning approaches that are especially effective for pattern recognition, classification, regression, and other complicated data-driven tasks. Here's a breakdown of neural networks:

1. **The Fundamental Structure**:

A neural network is made up of linked nodes or neurons that are grouped into layers. The three primary levels are as follows:

- **Input Layer**: This layer is where the first data or features are received.

- **Hidden Layers**: These intermediate layers process the incoming data using weighted connections and non-linear activation functions.

- **Output Layer**: This layer generates the final result, which might be a classification, regression prediction, or another task-specific outcome.

2. Nodes (Neurons):

- In a neural network, each neuron performs a basic computation. It receives input from several neurons in the preceding layer, assigns a weight to each input, adds them all together, and then sends the result through an activation function.

- The weights indicate the strength of neural connections and are learnt during training to improve the network's performance.

3. Functions of Activation:

- Activation functions add nonlinearity to the network, allowing it to simulate complicated data interactions. The following are examples of common activation functions:

- **Sigmoid**: Produces values ranging from 0 to 1, and is frequently employed in binary classification tasks.

- **ReLU (Rectified Linear Unit):** A deep learning unit that outputs the input for positive values and zero for negative values.

- **Tanh (Hyperbolic Tangent):** Produces results ranging from -1 to 1, similar to sigmoid but centred on zero.

4. Feedback Process:

- Data passes from the input layer to the output layer via the hidden layers during the feedforward process. Each layer's neurons calculate their outputs based on the inputs they receive and the learnt weights.

- The output layer's ultimate output is utilized to make predictions or choices.

5. Training (Education):

- Neural networks learn from data via a process known as training. The weights of the connections between neurons are adjusted to minimize the discrepancy between the expected output and the actual goal values.

Backpropagation and derivatives such as stochastic gradient descent (SGD) and Adam are common training methods.

6. DNNs (Deep Neural Networks):

Deep neural networks are neural networks that include several hidden layers. They have revolutionized disciplines such as image recognition and natural language processing by being particularly good at learning hierarchical features from data.

- "Deep learning" refers to the application of deep neural networks.

7. Applications:

- Neural networks have several uses, including:
- Recognition of images and speech
- NLP (natural language processing)
- Self-driving cars
- Playing video games (for example, AlphaGo)
- Healthcare (for example, illness diagnosis)
- Financial forecasting and modelling
- Recommendation systems

8. **Difficulties and Considerations**:

- Deep neural network training can be computationally costly and need vast volumes of labelled data.

- Overfitting (model fitting noise in training data) is a typical problem, demanding regularization approaches.

- When deploying neural networks, ethical issues, transparency, and interpretability are vital, especially in key fields.

Ensemble Methods:

Ensemble techniques are sophisticated machine learning and data mining tools that integrate predictions or judgments from numerous different models to generate a stronger and more accurate final model. These strategies are especially useful when individual models have varying strengths and limitations. The goal of ensemble approaches is to decrease the danger of overfitting, increase generalization, and improve prediction performance.

There are various common ensemble approaches, with two major categories:

1. Bagging (Bootstrap Aggregation):

- **Random Forest**: One of the most well-known ensemble approaches is Random Forest. During training, it generates numerous decision trees, each with a distinct subset of the training data and a subset of the features. The ultimate forecast is produced by averaging or voting on all of the different trees' projections. This decreases overfitting while increasing robustness.

- **Bagged Decision Trees**: Bagging, like Random Forest, may be used in various base models besides decision trees. It entails training numerous models on distinct random samples of data (with replacement) and then averaging their predictions.

2. Boosting:

- **AdaBoost (Adaptive Boosting):** AdaBoost is an iterative ensemble algorithm that prioritizes misclassified occurrences with each iteration. It gives misclassified data points larger weights and trains a new weak learner to remedy these errors. It continues this procedure for a certain number of iterations, and the final prediction is a weighted mixture of the predictions of the weak learners.

- **Gradient Boosting Machines (GBM)**: Another common boosting approach is GBM. It successively constructs an ensemble of decision trees. Each tree is educated to rectify the mistakes committed by the ones before it. To minimize a loss function, GBM employs a gradient descent optimization technique.

- **XGBoost, LightGBM, and CatBoost**: These are optimized and efficient gradient-boosting solutions that have grown in popularity in recent years. They improve speed and performance and are commonly utilized in machine-learning contests and real-world applications.

Ensemble approaches have various advantages:

- **Improved Accuracy**: Because ensembles integrate the characteristics of numerous models, they often outperform individual models in terms of predictive performance.

- **Reduced Overfitting**: Ensemble techniques can decrease overfitting by aggregating predictions from various models. Overfitting can arise when a single model is overly complicated.

- **Robustness**: Ensembles are more resistant to data noise and outliers since mistakes or abnormalities in individual models may be compensated for by others.

- **Model Interpretability**: Certain ensemble approaches, such as Random Forest, can shed light on feature relevance and model behaviour.

- **Variability**: Ensemble techniques may be applied to a variety of basic models, making them adaptable to a variety of machine learning problems.

However, there are several considerations for ensemble methods:

- **Computational Cost:** Creating and training numerous models can be computationally expensive, especially when dealing with huge datasets.

- **Parameter adjustment**: Ensembles frequently need hyperparameter adjustment, which may be time-consuming.

- **Interpretability**: When compared to simpler models, some ensemble approaches, particularly those with a high number of base models, might be difficult to read.

6

Chapter 6: Model Evaluation and Validation

Data for Training and Testing:

Data for training and testing is critical in the machine learning and data mining processes. They are critical in the development and evaluation of prediction models. The following is an explanation of training and testing data:

1. Training Information:

- **Purpose**: A machine learning or data mining model is trained using training data. The model learns patterns, correlations, and linkages in the data during the training phase so that it can make predictions or classifications on fresh, unknown data.

- **Materials**: A dataset with established outcomes or labels is used as training data. It incorporates both input features (variables or characteristics) and their matching target values or labels in supervised learning.

- **Procedure:** The model examines the training data and modifies its internal parameters or decision limits to suit the data patterns. In neural networks, this process incorporates optimization methods such as gradient descent or backpropagation.

- **Size**: The amount of training data is crucial. Larger, more diversified training datasets frequently result in more accurate and resilient models.

2. Testing Data (Test Data or Validation Data):

- **Purpose**: Testing data is used to evaluate a trained model's performance and generalization capabilities. It enables you to assess how well the model will perform on previously unknown real-world data.

- **Materials**: Testing data, like training data, contains input characteristics, but the labels or goal values are concealed from the model during testing. This is necessary for simulating real-world circumstances in which you must predict outcomes without prior knowledge.

- **Process**: Based on the patterns learnt during training, the trained model makes predictions on the testing data. To assess the model's accuracy and performance, these predictions are compared to the real, withheld labels.

- **Separation:** The original dataset is often separated into two subsets: the training set (for model training) and the testing set (for assessment). Depending on the facts provided, common divisions include 70-30, 80-20, or 90-10.

3. Optional Cross-Validation:

- **Purpose:** Cross-validation is used in some circumstances instead of a separate testing dataset. Cross-validation techniques divide the dataset into numerous subsets or "folds," which are then used as both training and testing data iteratively. This contributes to a more robust evaluation of the model's performance.

 - **K-Fold Cross-Validation**: Cross-validation is commonly performed by splitting the data into K equally-sized folds, training the model on K-1 folds, and then testing it on the remaining fold. This procedure is done K times, with each fold acting as a test set just once. To evaluate overall performance, the results are averaged.

Cross-Validation:

Cross-validation is an important approach in machine learning and data analysis for assessing a prediction model's performance and generalization capabilities. It is used to predict how well a model will perform on unknown data, which is critical for ensuring that the model does neither overfit nor underfit the training data. Cross-validation entails splitting the dataset into many subgroups and then training and testing the model on various combinations of these subsets. K-fold cross-validation is the most prevalent type of cross-validation.

<u>Here's how k-fold cross-validation works:</u>

1. **Data Splitting**: The dataset is separated into k equal-sized, non-overlapping "folds." For example, if you select k = 5, your dataset will be divided into five sections known as Fold 1, Fold 2, Fold 3, Fold 4, and Fold 5.

2. **Model Training and Testing**: The training and testing procedure is repeated k times, each time with a different fold serving as the test set and the remaining k-1 folds serving as the training set.

3. **Performance Evaluation**: You evaluate the model's performance on the test set after each iteration. Depending on whether the challenge is classification or regression, common performance indicators include accuracy, precision, recall, F1-score, and mean squared error.

4. **Average Performance**: After completing all k iterations, you compute the average performance measure (e.g., average accuracy) over all iterations. A single train-test split offers a less stable assessment of the model's performance.

Benefits of Cross-Validation:

- **Robust Performance Estimation**: Cross-validation delivers a more trustworthy assessment of a model's performance by testing and training on numerous subsets of data, decreasing the influence of data variability.

- **Prevents Overfitting**: Because the model is tested on several test sets, it ensures that it generalizes effectively to previously unknown data.

- **Utilizes All Data Points**: All data points are utilised for both training and testing, which is especially significant when the dataset is small.

Common Cross-Validation Variations:

1. **Stratified K-Fold Cross-Validation:** This variant assures that each fold retains the same class distribution as the original dataset in classification problems with unbalanced class distribution.

2. **Leave-One-Out Cross-Validation**: In LOOCV, k is set to the number of data points in the dataset, implying that each data point is used as a test set once and then utilized for training the rest of the time.

3. **Time Series Cross-Validation**: For time series data, the sequence of data points is important. It guarantees that previous data is utilized for training and future data is used for testing.

Metrics of Evaluation (Accuracy, Precision, Recall, F1-Score, and so on):

In data mining and machine learning, evaluation metrics are critical tools for assessing the effectiveness of prediction models and algorithms. These metrics assist you in understanding how well your model performs in terms of producing proper predictions and managing various parts of data categorization and regression. Here's a breakdown of several standard assessment measures, such as Accuracy, Precision, Recall, and F1-Score:

1. Accuracy:

- **Definition**: Accuracy is a measure of how many of your model's predictions were right out of all forecasts produced.

- **Calculation**: (Total Number of Predictions / (Number of Correct Predictions).

- **Application**: When you have an approximately balanced class distribution (i.e., the number of samples in each class is nearly equal), accuracy provides a simple statistic for overall model performance. When dealing with skewed datasets, however, it can be deceptive.

2. Precision:

- **Definition**: Precision is the fraction of genuine positive predictions (properly predicted positives) that the model makes out of all positive predictions.

- **Calculation**: (True Positives + False Positives) / (True Positives + False Positives)

- **Use Case**: When the cost of false positives is large, precision is critical. For example, in medical diagnostics, you want to avoid needless treatments by minimizing false positives.

3. Recall (also known as Sensitivity or True Positive Rate):

- **Definition**: Recall is the fraction of accurate positive predictions in a dataset out of all real positive cases.

- **Calculation:** (True Positives) / (False Negatives + True Positives)

- **Application**: When missing genuine positives is costly, recall is critical. In spam email detection, for example, you want to catch as many spam emails as possible, even if it entails some false alarms.

4. F1-Score:

- **Definition**: The harmonic mean of accuracy and recall is the F1-Score. It gives a fair assessment of a model's performance by accounting for both false positives and erroneous negatives.

- **Calculation:** *Use Case: 2 (Precision Recall) / (Precision + Recall)* The F1-Score is especially useful when accuracy and recall must be balanced, there is an uneven class distribution, or false positives and false negatives have distinct meanings.

5. Specificity (genuine Negative Rate):

- **Definition**: Specificity is the fraction of genuine negative predictions in the dataset compared to all real negative cases.

- **Calculation:** (True Negatives) / (False Positives + True Negatives)

- **Application**: Specificity is significant in circumstances when recognizing real negatives is critical, such as medical testing where a negative result implies the absence of a disease.

6. ROC Curve and AUC:

- **Definition:** The Receiver Operating Characteristic (ROC) curve depicts a classifier's performance over multiple thresholds. The Area Under the ROC Curve (AUC) measures the model's overall performance.

- **Application:** ROC curves are useful for visualizing and comparing the trade-offs between true positive rate and false positive rate at various categorization levels.

Underfitting and Overfitting:

**Overfitting**:

Overfitting happens when a model learns the training data so well that it retains not just the underlying patterns but also the noise and random oscillations. As a result, an overfit model performs exceptionally well on training data but poorly on fresh, previously unknown data. Overfitting is frequently characterized by the following characteristics:

1. **High Test Accuracy, Low Training Accuracy**: On training data, the model obtains high accuracy or a low error rate, but performs badly on validation or test data.

2. **Complex Models**: Overfit models are typically extremely complicated, having an excessive number of parameters or variables. They can account for even the noise in the data.

3. **Generalization Issues**: Because the model has effectively memorized the training data, it fails to generalize its predictions to new, unknown data.

4. **High Variance**: Overfit models have a high variance, which means they are sensitive to modest changes in training data, resulting in different outputs when the data is slightly changed.

**Underfitting**:

In contrast, underfitting happens when a model is too simplistic to capture the underlying patterns in the data. In this example, the model fails to understand essential correlations and performs badly on both the training and fresh data sets. Underfitting is distinguished by:

1. **Low Test Accuracy, Low Training Accuracy**: The model fails to perform effectively on either training or fresh data. It is characterized by excessive mistakes and low precision.

2. **Overly simple Models**: Underfit models are overly simple and may lack the complexities needed to capture the subtleties in the data.

3. **Biased Predictions**: The model produces biased or excessively broad predictions that fail to appropriately represent the underlying data distribution.

4. **High Bias:** Underfit models have a high bias, which means they make incorrect assumptions about the data.

How to Balance Overfitting and Underfitting:

The objective of machine learning is to achieve high model performance on fresh, unseen data by striking a balance between overfitting and underfitting. This is sometimes referred to as "model generalization." Among the techniques for achieving this equilibrium are:

1. **Cross-validation**: Use techniques like as k-fold cross-validation to see how well your model generalizes to previously unknown data.

2. **Feature Selection**: To decrease complexity, remove unnecessary or redundant features from your model.

3. **Regularization**: Use regularization techniques such as L1 (Lasso) or L2 (Ridge) regularization to penalize big model parameters and therefore reduce model complexity.

4. **Ensemble Methods**: Combining different models can help to prevent overfitting. Techniques like bagging and boosting can help with generalization.

5. **Collect More Information**: More data can sometimes help a model generalize better, especially when overfitting is an issue owing to a short dataset.

7

Chapter 7: Feature Selection and Engineering

Techniques for Feature Selection:

Feature selection is an important stage in machine learning and data mining data preparation. It entails selecting a subset of relevant characteristics (variables or attributes) from the original collection of features to be used in the construction of a predictive model. There are various reasons why feature selection is important:

1. **Model Simplification**: Removing unnecessary or superfluous characteristics simplifies the model, which can result in improved model performance, less overfitting, and greater interpretability.

2. **Reducing Computational Complexity**: Fewer features mean less computational overhead, which is especially important when dealing with huge datasets.

3. Improving Model Generalization: Feature selection can assist in increasing a model's capacity to generalize to previously unknown data by focusing on the most useful attributes.

4. Avoiding the Dimensionality Curse: The number of characteristics in high-dimensional spaces can rise exponentially, making it difficult to train appropriate models. This issue is mitigated by feature selection.

Here are a few examples of typical feature selection techniques:

1. Filter Methods:

- **Feature Selection Based on Correlation**: This approach ranks features according to their relationship to the target variable. Features having a strong correlation are kept.

    - **Chi-Square Experiment**: It assesses the dependency between each characteristic and the goal and is best suited for categorical target variables.

    - **Mutual Information:** The amount of information that one characteristic offers about another or the goal variable.

2. Wrapper Methods:

- **RFE (Recursive Feature Elimination)**: This approach eliminates the least significant feature(s) recursively and trains the model on the remaining features until a given number of features are attained or a performance measure is optimized.

- **Forward Selection**: Begin with an empty collection of features and add one at a time, picking the one that has the greatest impact on model performance.

- **Backward Elimination**: Starts with all features and eliminates the one that is least relevant in each iteration until a stopping condition is reached.

3. Embedded Methods:

- **L1 Regularization (Lasso)**: Adds a penalty component to the cost function of the model, encouraging feature coefficients to be absolutely zero. The features with non-zero coefficients are chosen.

- **Tree-Based Approaches**: To assess feature relevance, decision trees and ensemble approaches such as Random Forest can be employed. Features that are regularly employed for node splitting are deemed more essential.

4. Hybrid Methods: Choose KBest with Machine Learning Algorithm: To iteratively enhance feature selection, you may combine filter techniques like SelectKBest (which selects the top k features based on statistical tests) with a machine learning algorithm.

5. **Domain Knowledge**: Domain knowledge and expert intuition can play an important role in feature selection. Experts in a certain field may provide insights regarding which characteristics are likely to be significant for a specific challenge.

6. **Feature significance Scores**: Certain algorithms, such as Random Forest and Gradient Boosting, may directly provide feature significance scores, which can be used to guide feature selection.

Methods of Feature Engineering:

Feature engineering is a critical stage in machine learning and data mining data preparation. It entails picking, altering, or producing additional features (input variables or characteristics) from raw data to improve machine learning model performance. Improved model accuracy, interpretability, and generalization may be achieved by effective feature engineering. Here are some examples of typical feature engineering techniques:

1. Filter Methods:

- **Feature Selection**: These approaches choose characteristics using statistical metrics such as correlation, chi-squared tests, or mutual information. They aid in the identification of the most important properties of the target variable.

- **Wrapper Techniques**: Wrapper approaches analyze the performance of feature subsets using machine learning models. Forward selection, backward elimination, and recursive feature elimination (RFE) are all common strategies.

2. Feature Transformation:

- **Scaling**: Scaling features to a consistent range (e.g., normalization or standardization) might increase the performance of distance-based algorithms (e.g., K-means).

- **Log Transformation**: When applied to skewed data, logarithmic transformations can make it more regularly distributed, which is useful for some algorithms.

- **Box-Cox Transformation**: Box-Cox changes data, similar to log transformation, to stabilize variances and make it more regularly distributed.

- **Polynomial Features**: Creating polynomial features (for example, by squaring or cubing existing features) might help to capture nonlinear connections in data.

3. Feature Creation:

- **Binning or Discretization**: Grouping continuous values into bins or categories might assist models in catching nonlinear patterns by simplifying the data.

- **Interaction Features**: Combining two or more existing features to create new features might capture interactions that individual features may not disclose.

- **Time-Based Features:** Extracting features from timestamps, such as weekday, month, or year, might assist models in capturing seasonality or temporal trends.

4. **Feature Encoding**: Converting categorical variables into binary (0/1) vectors for machine learning algorithms that require numerical input.

- **Label Encoding**: When ordinal variables have an intrinsic order, unique number labels to categories.

- **Target Encoding**: Encoding categorical variables depending on the value of the mean or target variable for each category, which can record connections between categories and the target.

5. Feature Imputation:

- **Handling Missing Data**: Using approaches such as mean imputation, median imputation, or more complex methods such as k-nearest neighbours imputation to fill in missing data.

- **Min-Max Scaling**: Scaling features to a certain range, commonly between 0 and 1.

- **Standardization**: Scaling features to have a mean of 0 and a standard deviation of 1.

7. Feature Extraction:

- **Principal Component Analysis (PCA)**: Data is reduced in dimensionality by converting it into a new collection of orthogonal variables (principal components) that capture the most relevant information.

- **Autoencoders**: Deep learning models that can learn compressed data representations to utilize as features.

8. **Text Feature Engineering**:

- To extract meaningful features from text data, techniques such as TF-IDF (Term Frequency-Inverse Document Frequency) and word embeddings (Word2Vec, GloVe) can be utilized.

Dimensionality Reduction:

Dimensionality reduction is an important approach in data analysis and machine learning. It entails removing as many characteristics or variables as feasible from a dataset while maintaining as much valuable information as possible. This approach may be very useful in a variety of contexts, including boosting model efficiency, lowering computing complexity, and improving data interpretability. A more extensive description of dimensionality reduction follows:

Why Dimensionality Reduction is Required:

1. **The Dimensionality Curse**: The volume of the feature space expands exponentially as the number of features in a dataset increases. This might result in data sparsity, higher computing needs, and difficulty seeing and comprehending data.

2. **Excessive Fitting**: Overfitting is more likely with large datasets. Models may perform well on training data but perform badly on unknown data because they have effectively remembered the data's noise.

3. **Dimensionality Reduction Objectives**:
   1. **Simplify Data**: Reduce the dataset's complexity by removing unnecessary or duplicate information, making it easier to analyze.

2. **Visualization:** Project high-dimensional data into a lower-dimensional area to more effectively view and understand it.

3. **Computational Efficiency**: Lower the computational cost and time necessary to train and evaluate machine learning models.

4. **Better Generalization**: Reduce overfitting and increase a model's capacity to generalize to new, previously unknown data.

Methods for Reducing Dimensionality:

1. **Feature Choice**: In feature selection, you choose a subset of the most significant features while eliminating others that are less important. Typically, this is accomplished by ranking features based on criteria such as correlation, mutual information, or feature relevance ratings.

2. **Extraction of Features**: Techniques for extracting features generate new features, known as synthetic features or components, that capture the crucial information in the original data. Principal Component Analysis (PCA) and Linear Discriminant Analysis (LDA) are two popular approaches for feature extraction:

- **PCA (Principal Component Analysis):** PCA finds orthogonal axes (primary components) in data that maximize variance. It projects the data onto these components, allowing you to decrease the number of dimensions while retaining as much variation as feasible.

- **LDA (Linear Discriminant Analysis)**: In classification difficulties, LDA is frequently utilized. It finds linear feature combinations that enhance separation between classes while minimizing dimensionality.

3. **Manifold Learning**: Manifold learning approaches seek to retain the data's underlying structure. Lower-dimensional data representations with local associations between data points are created using methods such as t-distributed Stochastic Neighbor Embedding (t-SNE) and Isomap.

Thoughts on Dimensionality Reduction:

1. **Information Loss**: Dimensionality reduction invariably results in some information loss. The goal is to minimize this loss while attaining the necessary dimensionality reduction.

2. **Hyperparameter Tuning**: Some dimensionality reduction strategies need the adjustment of hyperparameters such as the amount of components or features to be retained. Cross-validation can aid in the discovery of optimal settings.

3. **Domain Expertise**: When determining which features to choose or how to do feature extraction, it is critical to understand the domain and context of the data.

4. **Impact on Model Performance**: Always assess the impact of dimensionality reduction on the performance of your machine learning models. Reduced dimensionality may increase model performance in some circumstances, but it may have a detrimental influence in others.

8

Chapter 8: Ethical Considerations in Data Mining

Privacy Issues:

Privacy concerns are an important component of data mining and the larger area of data science. They are concerned with the ethical and legal concerns surrounding the acquisition, use, and management of persons' personal information. Here's how to address privacy problems in the context of data mining:

1. Data Gathering and Consent:

- How data is acquired is one of the key privacy issues. Individuals are not always aware that their data is being gathered, and they may not have explicitly consented to its usage. This can result in a breach of trust and invasion of privacy.

2. **Data Anonymization**: Even when data is gathered with consent, the danger of de-anonymization exists. Even when personal

information has been stripped of direct identifiers, data mining techniques can occasionally disclose it. This presents a danger to privacy.

3. Data breaches and security failings can expose sensitive information to unauthorized parties. It is critical to protect data against theft and illegal access to ensure privacy.

4. **Discrimination and profiling**: Data mining can result in the development of comprehensive user profiles. While these profiles can be useful for a variety of objectives, they can also be abused to engage in discriminatory actions such as unjustly targeting certain groups or making judgments based on biased algorithms.

5. **Re-identification Attacks:** Attackers can use publicly accessible information to try to re-identify persons in allegedly anonymous databases. This may result in the disclosure of sensitive personal information.

6. **Surveillance and intrusion**: Data mining can be used for surveillance purposes by governments or commercial groups in some situations. This can violate a person's right to privacy and raise worries about mass monitoring.

7. **Lack of Transparency:** Individuals may not understand how their data is being utilized when data mining procedures are opaque, making it harder for them to exert control over their personal information.

8. **Legal and Regulatory Compliance**: - Privacy laws and regulations put legal requirements on enterprises for the collecting, storage, and processing of personal data, such as the European Union's General Data Protection Regulation (GDPR) and the California Consumer Privacy Act (CCPA). Noncompliance might result in severe penalties and legal repercussions.

9. **Data Retention and Deletion**: Individuals have the right to have their data deleted if it is no longer required for the purpose for which it was obtained. Organizations must put in place processes to respect these demands.

10. Making Informed Decisions:

- Privacy concerns also extend to people's capacity to make educated judgments about their data. They should be able to learn about the data being gathered and how it will be utilized.

Fairness and bias:

In data mining, machine learning, and artificial intelligence (AI), bias and fairness are key topics. They address the possibility of discrimination or unjust treatment of individuals or groups when algorithms make choices or predictions. In the context of data mining, here's an explanation of bias and fairness:

1. Bias:

The existence of systematic and unjust discrimination in data, algorithms, or decision-making processes is referred to as bias. Bias can appear in a variety of ways:

- **Information Bias**: The data used to train machine learning models might not be representative of the general population. Because the model learns on biased data, this might result in biased predictions. For example, if a facial recognition system is largely trained on photographs of light-skinned people, it may perform badly on images of people with darker skin tones.

- **Bias in Algorithms**: Algorithms can be biased if they are built or taught in such a manner that they consistently favour one group over another. This might happen if the training data is skewed or if discriminating characteristics are included in the model.

- **Bias in Outcome**: Even if algorithms are neutral, their results may be viewed as biased if they disproportionately harm particular groups. For example, a fair loan approval algorithm may nonetheless result in more denials for a specific demographic group due to past inequalities.

- **Bias of the User**: When humans engage with AI systems, they might add prejudice. Biased search searches, for example, might propagate preconceptions by resulting in biased suggestions from search engines or social media platforms.

2. Equity:

In data mining and machine learning, fairness refers to the objective of treating all persons or groups equally and without prejudice. To achieve fairness, prejudice must be reduced or eliminated so that algorithms and judgments do not disproportionately hurt or favour any one group. There are several definitions and strategies for fairness, such as:

- **Demographic Fairness**: Ensuring that an algorithm's predictions or judgments do not differ considerably across demographic groupings such as race, gender, age, or socioeconomic position.

- **Individual Fairness**: Treating comparable people in the same way, regardless of group membership. This method focuses on creating predictions or judgments for persons with comparable traits.

- **Equal Opportunity:** Ensuring that the algorithm gives persons with equivalent credentials or traits, regardless of their background, equal chances, such as job interviews or loan approvals.

- **Counterfactual Fairness**: Evaluating fairness by analyzing alternate situations in which people's qualities are modified to see how the algorithm's conclusions are influenced.

Accountability and transparency:

Transparency and accountability are two key concepts in data mining, especially when it comes to handling and analyzing data, particularly sensitive or personal information. These principles are critical for ensuring that data mining tools are used responsibly and ethically.

1. Transparency:

Transparency in data mining refers to the technique of making the whole data mining process as visible and intelligible to important stakeholders as feasible, from data collection to model building and deployment. It entails offering insights into the data mining process's processes, algorithms, and judgments. The following are important characteristics of data mining transparency:

- **Data Collection and Source**: Clearly stating the source of the data and how it was gathered. This contains information about the data's origins, gathering techniques, and any biases.

- **Data Preprocessing**: Recording the procedures taken to clean, convert, and preprocess data. This guarantees that others can replicate the same preparation methods and understand the quality of the data.

- **Algorithm Selection**: Explaining why various data mining algorithms were chosen for a given purpose. This involves debating the benefits and drawbacks of various algorithms.

- **Model Creation**: Transparency into model training, including hyperparameter selection and model architecture. This explains how predictions are made to others.

- **Evaluation Metrics**: State the evaluation metrics that were used to measure the model's performance. Transparency here guarantees that the success criteria are well-defined.

- **Bias and Fairness:** Addressing and documenting any possible biases in data or models, as well as initiatives for bias reduction. Transparency is essential for recognizing and correcting unfair or discriminatory outcomes.

- **Data Privacy:** Making certain that sensitive and personally identifiable information is handled with care and by privacy rules. Transparency entails reporting data security safeguards in place.

2. Accountability:

Data mining accountability is directly tied to responsibility and ethical behaviour. Individuals and organizations must be held accountable for their activities throughout the data mining process. The following are important characteristics of data mining accountability:

- **Data Ownership and Stewardship**: Determining who owns the data, who is responsible for its upkeep, and who is held liable for data breaches or abuse.

- **Ethical norms**: Following recognized ethical norms and principles for data mining, such as those concerning privacy, consent, and fairness.

- **Regulatory Compliance**: Ensuring that data mining operations adhere to appropriate legal and regulatory frameworks, such as

GDPR (General Data Protection Regulation) in Europe or HIPAA (Health Insurance Portability and Accountability Act) in the United States.

- **Documentation**: Keeping detailed records of data mining operations, choices, and procedures. This paperwork is beneficial during audits and inquiries.

- **Accountability for Results**: Individuals and organizations must be held accountable for the consequences of data mining efforts, including any harm caused by inaccurate forecasts or misapplication of information.

- **Continuous Monitoring**: Monitoring and reviewing the impact of data mining models regularly and making required modifications to maintain fairness, accuracy, and compliance.

9

Chapter 9: Future Trends in Data Mining

Data Mining and Big Data:

Big Data and Data Mining are two interrelated topics in data analytics, both of which play critical roles in extracting useful insights and information from large and complicated datasets. Here's a breakdown of each:

Large Data:

Big Data refers to extraordinarily massive and complicated datasets that are inefficiently handled by typical data processing tools and methodologies. These datasets are distinguished by three Vs:

1. **Size**: Massive volumes of data are involved in Big Data. This information might originate from a variety of sources, such as social media, sensors, commercial transactions, and more. The size of the volume might vary from terabytes to petabytes and beyond.

2. **Speed**: Data is being produced and gathered at an unprecedented rate. Social media sites, for example, generate a continuous stream of data in real-time, while IoT (Internet of Things) devices continually generate data. Velocity emphasizes the need to process data swiftly to get timely insights.

3. **Diversity**: Big Data encompasses a wide range of data types, including structured data (e.g., databases), semi-structured data (e.g., XML files), unstructured data (e.g., text, photos, videos), and others. Managing and analyzing such a wide range of data types presents a substantial difficulty.

4. **Authenticity:** The dependability of data is referred to as its veracity. Big Data frequently contains noisy or partial information, therefore data quality is an issue.

5. **Value**: Working with Big Data has the ultimate objective of extracting useful insights and knowledge that may drive informed decision-making, enhance processes, and generate competitive advantages.

Organizations use specialized technologies and tools such as Hadoop, Spark, NoSQL databases, and distributed computing frameworks to handle and analyze Big Data. Big Data analytics strategies concentrate on extracting patterns, trends, correlations, and useful information from enormous databases.

Information Mining:

The process of uncovering patterns, correlations, and meaningful information from data is known as data mining. It entails sifting through data, identifying hidden patterns, and extracting knowledge using various algorithms and methodologies. The field of data mining is a subset of the larger area of machine learning and artificial intelligence.

Data Mining fundamental ideas include:

1. **Data Preprocessing**: Cleaning and preparing data for analysis by dealing with missing values, and outliers, and translating data into a suitable format.

2. **EDA (Exploratory Data Analysis)**: Data visualization and summarization are used in EDA to acquire a basic grasp of its features.

3. **Data Mining Methods**: Classification, clustering, regression, association rule mining, and anomaly detection are some of the

techniques used in data mining. These strategies aid in the resolution of various sorts of difficulties.

4. **Model Assessment:** It is critical to evaluate the performance of Data Mining models to ensure their correctness and dependability. Accuracy, precision, recall, and F1-score are all common assessment criteria.

5. **Feature Selection and Design**: These methods entail selecting the most relevant variables (features) for analysis as well as developing additional features to improve model performance.

6. **Practical Applications**: Customer segmentation, fraud detection, recommendation systems, and predictive maintenance are just a few of the businesses that use data mining.

Integration of AI and Machine Learning:

The combination of artificial intelligence (AI) and machine learning (ML) provides a tremendous synergy with the potential to change a wide range of industries and applications. Here's an explanation of the merging of AI and machine learning:

1. AI and Machine Learning Fundamentals:

- **Artificial Intelligence (AI)**: Artificial intelligence (AI) is a vast subject of computer science that tries to construct robots or systems capable of doing activities that normally require human intelligence. Problem-solving, decision-making, natural language processing, and perception are examples of these activities.

- **Machine Learning (ML)**: ML is a subset of artificial intelligence that focuses on building algorithms and models that allow computers to learn from data and make predictions or judgments without being explicitly programmed. With time and data, machine learning algorithms enhance their performance.

2. AI and Machine Learning Integration:

- AI and ML are frequently combined to improve the capabilities of AI systems. This integration entails the use of machine learning techniques to enable AI systems to learn and adapt to new data and scenarios. The following is how integration works:

3. Data-Informed Decision Making:

- Machine learning is critical to AI's ability to make data-driven judgments. ML algorithms are used by AI systems to examine massive datasets, identify patterns, and make predictions or suggestions based on this analysis.

- In a recommendation system, for example, AI can utilize ML to study a user's prior behaviour and preferences to offer items, movies, or content they would like.

4. Adaptive Learning:

ML-enabled AI systems may adapt and enhance their performance over time. They are always learning from new facts and adjusting their behaviour as a result.

- In self-driving cars, for example, AI combined with ML may learn from real-world driving scenarios to enhance navigation and safety.

5. **Natural Language Understanding**: ML approaches are critical in natural language processing (NLP), an area of artificial intelligence. NLP enables AI systems to comprehend and produce human language.

- Chatbots and virtual assistants like Siri and Alexa employ machine learning models to comprehend and reply to spoken or written language.

6. **Computer Vision**: Machine learning is essential in computer vision applications. It helps artificial intelligence systems to detect and understand visual data such as photographs and movies.

- AI-ML integration in computer vision may be seen in facial recognition systems, picture categorization, and object identification.

7. **Predictive Analytics**: ML models are used by AI systems for predictive analytics. Based on previous data, they can anticipate future events, trends, or results.

- AI-ML integration is utilized in finance for stock price prediction and risk assessment.

8. Healthcare and Medicine:

- The combination of AI and machine learning is altering healthcare by enhancing diagnostics, medication development, and patient care. Medical data, such as medical scans or patient information, are analyzed by ML models to produce accurate predictions and aid healthcare providers.

9. Difficulties and Considerations:

- While AI-ML integration has enormous promise, it also raises concerns about data quality, bias, ethics, and transparency. When designing AI-ML systems, it is critical to address these concerns properly.

Data Mining's Role in Industry 4.0:

Data mining plays a vital and transformational role in Industry 4.0, often known as the Fourth Industrial Revolution. Industry 4.0 denotes a new age of industrial production that incorporates digital technology, automation, the Internet of Things (IoT), and artificial intelligence (AI) into numerous industrial processes. In the following respects, data mining is critical to this transformation:

1. **Decision-Making Based on Data**: Data-driven decision-making is central to Industry 4.0. Data mining techniques are used to extract important insights and patterns from massive amounts of data supplied by sensors, machines, and other Internet of Things devices. These insights allow businesses to make more informed decisions regarding production, maintenance, and resource allocation.

2. **Predictive Maintenance**: Predictive maintenance is a fundamental use of data mining in Industry 4.0. Data mining algorithms can forecast when machinery may fail by evaluating past data on equipment performance and sensor readings. This enables firms to plan maintenance actions, decreasing downtime and increasing overall efficiency.

3. Data mining may be used to monitor and optimize industrial operations. Manufacturers can detect faults, departures from ideal

conditions, and other concerns in real-time by evaluating data from sensors and cameras. This data may be utilized to make real-time adjustments to operations, enhancing product quality and decreasing waste.

4. **Supply Chain Optimization**: By examining data on inventory levels, demand projections, transportation routes, and other factors, data mining may assist in improving the supply chain. This helps enterprises to cut costs, shorten lead times, and ensure items are delivered on time to clients.

5. **Customization and personalisation**: Product customization and personalisation are enhanced by Industry 4.0. Data mining aids in the collection and analysis of consumer data to better understand client preferences and purchasing behaviour. This data is utilized to personalize products and services to the specific demands of each consumer.

6. **Energy Efficiency**: Data mining techniques may be used to find potential for energy efficiency improvements in energy consumption data. This is critical for lowering the environmental effect of industrial processes while also lowering operating expenses.

7. **Supply and Demand Forecasting**: Data mining models can estimate future demand by analyzing previous sales data, industry patterns, and other factors. This is especially critical for effectively controlling inventory and production levels.

8. **Safety and Compliance**: Data mining may also be used for safety monitoring and regulatory compliance. Organizations may discover possible dangers and verify that safety standards are followed by evaluating data from safety sensors and cameras.

9. **Continuous Learning and Adaptation**: Systems in Industry 4.0 are dynamic and adaptive. Data mining models may learn from fresh data and adapt to changing situations in real-time, increasing their accuracy and efficacy over time.

10

Chapter 10: FAQs

1. What is data mining?

- Data mining is the process of discovering meaningful patterns, trends, or knowledge from large datasets using various techniques and algorithms.

2. Why is data mining important?

- Data mining helps organizations make informed decisions, identify hidden insights, and improve operations, leading to better business outcomes.

3. What types of data can be used for data mining?

- Data mining can be applied to various data types, including structured data (e.g., databases), unstructured data (e.g., text), and semi-structured data (e.g., XML).

4. What are some common applications of data mining?

- Common applications include customer segmentation, fraud detection, recommendation systems, and predictive analytics.

5. What is the difference between supervised and unsupervised learning in data mining?

- Supervised learning uses labelled data for training, while unsupervised learning explores data without predefined labels.

6. What is overfitting in data mining?

- Overfitting occurs when a model learns noise in the data rather than the underlying patterns, leading to poor generalization.

7. What are some data mining tools and software for beginners?

- Popular tools include Python libraries (e.g., Scikit-Learn), R, and data mining software like RapidMiner and Weka.

8. How do I choose the right algorithm for my data mining project?

- Consider your data type and problem type. Start with simple algorithms and gradually explore more complex ones based on results.

9. What is feature engineering in data mining?

- Feature engineering involves selecting, creating, or transforming features (variables) to improve model performance.

10. Can data mining be applied to small datasets?

- Yes, data mining can be applied to small datasets, but it is often more effective with larger datasets due to increased patterns and insights.

11. What are some ethical considerations in data mining?

- Ethical concerns include privacy, bias, transparency, and accountability in data collection, analysis, and decision-making.

12. Is data mining the same as machine learning?

- Data mining is a broader field that encompasses machine learning. Machine learning is a subset of data mining focused on building predictive models.

13. How can I learn data mining as a beginner?

- Start with online courses, tutorials, and textbooks. Practice on small projects and gradually work on more complex datasets.

14. What are some common data preprocessing techniques in data mining?

- Data preprocessing includes data cleaning (removing errors), transformation (scaling features), and handling missing data.

15. What are some real-world examples of data mining success stories?

- Examples include Netflix's recommendation system, Amazon's product recommendations, and credit card fraud detection systems.

11

Conclusion

As we draw the curtains on our exploration of the captivating realm of data mining, you, dear reader, have embarked on a transformative journey. You've delved into the depths of data, uncovered hidden treasures, and harnessed the power of algorithms to make sense of the information-rich world around you. In this concluding chapter, let us reflect on the profound significance of your voyage into data mining for beginners.

Data mining is not just a technical endeavour; it is a gateway to understanding the complex tapestry of our modern world. It is the key that unlocks the mysteries concealed within vast datasets, revealing patterns, insights, and knowledge that were once obscured from view. By gaining proficiency in data mining, you have armed yourself with a potent tool that empowers you to make informed decisions, solve real-world problems, and drive positive change.

Throughout this book, you've learned about the fundamental concepts of data mining, from data collection and preparation to the intricacies of various algorithms and techniques. You've witnessed the magic of data visualization, the elegance of feature engineering, and the importance of ethical considerations in this data-driven age. You've seen how data mining can transform industries, enrich our lives, and pave the way for a brighter, more connected future.

As you continue your journey beyond these pages, remember that data mining is not a destination but a perpetual exploration. It is a field that evolves, adapts, and expands alongside the ever-growing sea of data. Embrace the curiosity that brought you here, and let it guide you to new horizons, new challenges, and discoveries.

In closing, let me share these heartfelt words with you: Data mining is a powerful tool, but its true potential lies in the hands of those who wield it responsibly, ethically, and with a thirst for knowledge. It is a journey that rewards not only the pursuit of answers but also the appreciation of questions. So, keep asking, keep exploring, and keep mining the rich seams of data that surround us, for therein lies the promise of a brighter and more informed future.

Thank you for embarking on this journey with us. May your path in data mining be illuminated by curiosity, guided by ethics, and filled with the joy of discovery. The world of data awaits your insights and contributions.

Safe travels on your data mining adventure, dear beginner. The future is yours to shape.

With warm regards,

Ernesto Cira